Fun With the Food Pyramid For Kids

#1 Children's Guide to Eating Whole Foods

USDA Nutritional Guidelines New Edition

by

George Roby and Nacim Khavarian

Illustrations by Drew Hofmann

AuthorHouse™
1663 Liberty Drive
Bloomington, IN 47403
www.authorhouse.com
Phone: 833-262-8899

This book is printed on acid-free paper.

ISBN: 978-1-4389-0914-1 (SC)

Library of Congress Control Number: 2008907635

Print information available on the last page.

Published by AuthorHouse 12/20/2023

authorHOUSE®

Introduction:

What is the food pyramid?

The food pyramid is a guide of what and how much you should eat per day in each food group.

There are six food groups that make up the pyramid.

1. The first group is **grains**: What are grains? Why do I need them? How much do I eat?

2. The second group is **vegetables**: What are vegetables? Why do I need them? How much do I eat?

3. The third group is **fruits**: What are fruits? Why do I need them? How much do I eat?

4. The fourth group is **dairy**: What is dairy? Why do I need them? How much do I eat?

5. The fifth group is **meats and beans**: What are meats & beans? Why do I need them? How much do I eat?

6. The sixth food group is **oils**. What are oils? Why do I need them?

7. Physical Activity. What is Physical Activity? Why is it important? How much is needed?

8. Life Tips and Things to Live By.

Why Know the Food Pyramid?

It's important to eat a variety of foods each day. The body, like a car, needs fuel. Food is fuel for people. Just like a car that doesn't run well when it gets the wrong kind of gas, a person may feel tired or sluggish or may become sick if he or she doesn't get the necessary nutrients.

THIS BOOK IS A GUIDE TO FIND YOUR BALANCE BETWEEN FOOD AND FUN.

FAT FACTS AND SUGAR SMARTS

Chapter 1: Grains Group

What is a Grain?

A grain is a single seed of cereal grass. Any food made from wheat, rice, oats, cornmeal, barley, or another cereal grain is a grain product. Bread, pasta, oatmeal, breakfast cereals, tortillas, and grits are examples of grain products.
There are two types of grains:

<u>Whole Grains</u>:
Whole grain examples are oatmeal, brown rice, and whole wheat flour.

<u>Refined Grains:</u>
Refined grain examples are white rice, white bread, and white flour.

Some grains grown in the U.S. are pictured below.

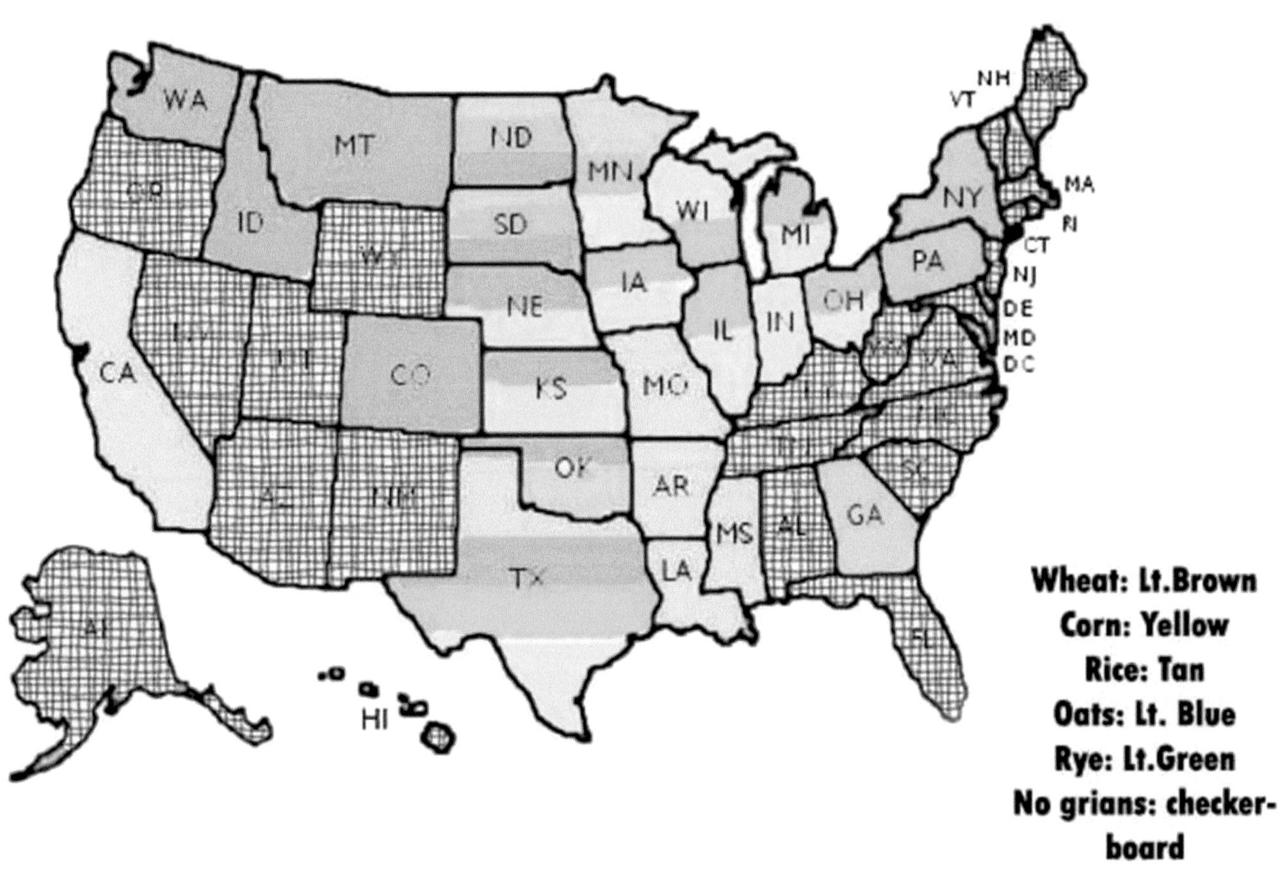

Why do I need grains?

Grains add delicious taste and variety to meals and are an important source of energy for the body. They also provide vitamins, minerals, and fiber to keep the body strong and healthy.

How much do I need?

The amount of grain you need depends on your age, gender, and physical activity. The portions below are recommended with thirty minutes or more each day of physical activity beyond your normal daily activities.

Children 4–8 years old = 4–5 ounces daily

Girls 9–13 years old = 5 ounces daily

Boys 9–13 years old = 6 ounces daily

At least half of all grains eaten should be whole grains. Below are some examples of 1-ounce portion sizes.

- 1 regular slice of bread
- 5 whole-wheat crackers
- ½ cup of whole-wheat pasta or 1 cup of cereal
- ½ cup cooked rice
- 3 cups of cooked popcorn

I am a food that is round with a hole in the middle. People eat me with jam, butter, or cream cheese. Some people make sandwiches out of me. What am I?

(Bagel)

Fun Snack Recipe:

<u>Crazy Crunch Mix</u>:
3 cups of Wheat Chex cereal
1½ cups of Cheerios
1 cup of pretzel strips
1 cup of cashews
1 cup of dark chocolate chips

Combine these ingredients together in a bowl and you have Crazy Crunch Mix!

I am made of flour. You can make sandwiches with me. I am a grain. What am I?

(Bread)

Chapter 2: Vegetables Group

A vegetable is any plant whose fruit, seeds, roots, bulbs, stems, leaves, or flower parts are used as food, such as the tomato, bean, potato, onion, spinach, and broccoli.
Vary Your Veggies. Go dark green and orange with your veggies. Eat spinach, broccoli, carrots, and sweet potatoes.

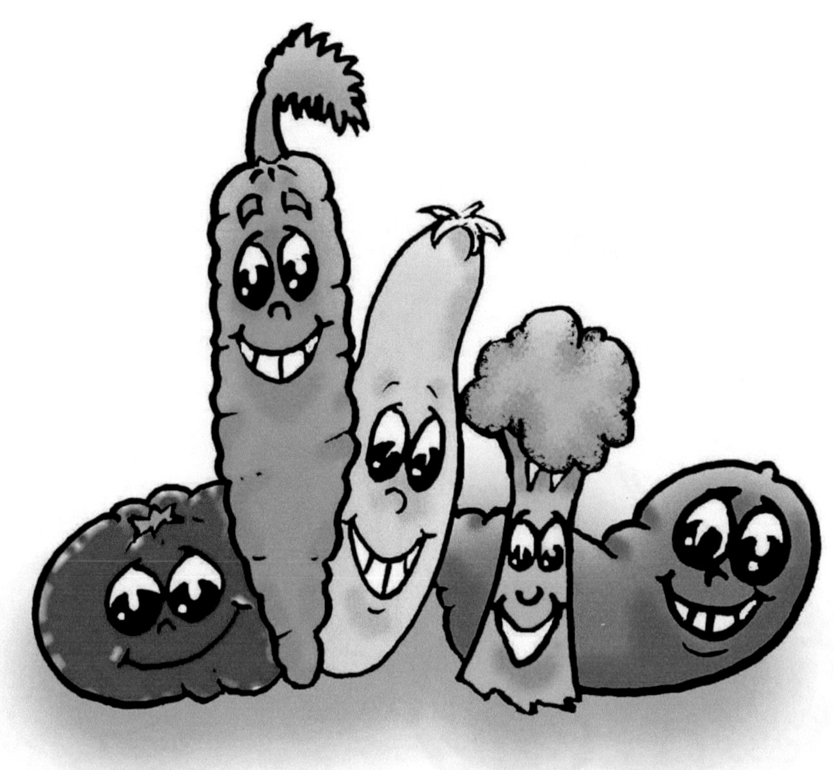

I have a skin with lots of layers. I can make your eyes water, and I grow in the garden. What am I?

(Onion)

How many vegetables should I eat per day?

Children: Ages 4–8 = 1 ½ cups

Girls: Ages 9–13 = 2 cups

Boys: Ages 9–13 = 2 ½ cups

In general, 1 cup of raw or cooked vegetables or vegetable juice, or 2 cups of raw leafy greens, can be considered as one cup from the vegetable group. Below are some examples of one-cup sizes in the vegetable group.

- 1 cup of chopped broccoli
- 1 cup of cooked spinach
- 1 large baked sweet potato
- 1 cup of corn
- 1 cup of green beans

I am a long, orange, pointy food. I am crunchy when you eat me raw. You can eat me with dip. What am I?

(Carrot)

Why should I eat vegetables?

Veggies provide nutrients vital for the health and maintenance of your body. Veggies provide important sources of nutrients, including potassium, fiber, and vitamins A, E, and C.

- Vitamin A keeps your eyes and skin healthy and helps your body protect against infections.

- Vitamin C helps heal cuts and wounds and keeps teach and gums clean.

- Vitamin E helps protect your cells against free radicals and unwanted pollutants

I am brown and I grow under the ground. You can bake me, mash me, or make fries from me. What am I?

(Potato)

Fun Snack Recipe:

<u>Spunky Vegetable Pizza</u>:
Ingredients:
¾ Cup Pizza Sauce
1 Large Italian pizza shell
1 Cup chopped broccoli
1 Cup shredded carrots
½ Cup sliced red or green bell pepper
5 to 6 ounces shredded, low-fat mozzarella or cheddar cheese

Directions:

1. Preheat oven to 450°F
2. Spoon pizza sauce on pizza shell
3. Place pizza shell on cookie sheet
4. Arrange vegetables over sauce
5. Sprinkle cheese over vegetables and sauce
6. Bake for 10 minutes
7. When baked, cool pizza for 3 minutes before slicing. Cut into 8 wedges.

Nutritional information:
Per serving: 236 calories, 13 g protein, 8 g fat (2 g Sat.), 29 g carbohydrates, 568 mg sodium, 15 mg cholesterol.

Chapter 3: Fruits Group

What is a fruit?

A fruit is similar to a vegetable in that it's any product that comes from a plant and is useful to humans and animals. The difference between veggies and fruits is that fruits are products of flowers and usually develop as a result of a flower being pollinated. However, some plants develop fruit without fertilization, and these fruits are seedless.

I am small brown food. My outside feels fuzzy. I am green inside and have tiny black seeds. What am I?

(Kiwi)

How do fruits grow?

There are three categories, as illustrated below; some fruits are grown from a bush, some are grown from trees, and others are grown from vines.

Vine	**Tree**	**Bush**
Grapes	Bananas	Blueberries
Pumpkins	Grapefruit	Rasberries
Strawberries	Pears	Pomegranates
Cantaloupes	Peaches	Black Berries
	Apples	
	Cherries	

I am long and yellow, and I grow in bunches on a tree. I am soft inside. You don't eat my outside. I taste sweet and yummy. What am I?

(Banana)

How much fruit should I eat a day?

As always, it depends on your age, gender, and physical activity. The portions below are recommended with thirty minutes or more each day of physical activity beyond your normal daily activities.

Serving sizes are:

Children 4–8 years old = 1 to 1½ cups

Girls 9–13 years old = 1½ cups

Boys 9–13 years old = 1½ cups

Below are examples of 1-cup serving sizes of fruits:

- 1 banana
- 1 large orange
- 1 large peach
- 32 seedless grapes
- 8 large strawberries

You can be safe with thinking of a baseball to estimate cup sizes.

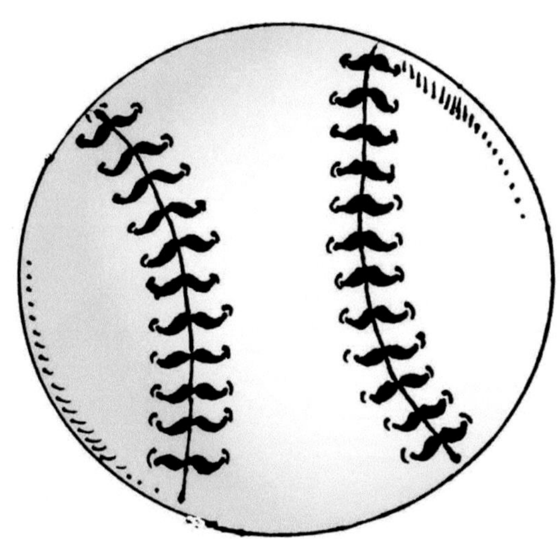

We grow in clumps on vines. We can be red, green, or purple. We taste sweet and can be squishy. What are we?

(Grapes)

Why do I need fruits?

Eating fruits provides many health benefits the body needs to be strong and active. Eating your recommended fruit servings daily helps your body fight unwanted infections and diseases.

Did you know?
The tomato is a fruit.

Fun Snack Recipe:

<u>Edible Art</u>

10 Canned or fresh pineapple rings or slices
5 Large bananas
2 Tangerines, segmented
1 Large apple, cut into small wedges
1 Pear, cut into small chunks
1 Kiwi, peeled and sliced (cut slices into halves or quarters)
Toothpicks

I am green, and when you cut me open, I am red. You eat me in the summertime. I am a fruit. What am I?

(Watermelon)

Chapter 4: Dairy or Milk Group

What's in the Dairy Group?

Dairy is comprised of all fluid milk products and many foods made from milk, such as yogurt and cheese.

How much of the dairy group should I have daily?
The amount you need daily depends on age.

Children 4–8 years old = 2 cups

Girls 9–13 years old = 3 cups

Boys 9–13 years old = 3 cups

Below are 1-cup portion-size equivalents:

- 1 cup of milk
- 1 8-oz container of yogurt
- 1 slice of cheese
- 1 cup of pudding

I am white and can be brown. I taste good cold. I come from cows and you can make butter, cheese, and chocolate from me. What am I?

(Milk)

Why is dairy important?

The dairy group contains calcium, which builds strong bones. Most milk-group choices should be fat free or low fat.

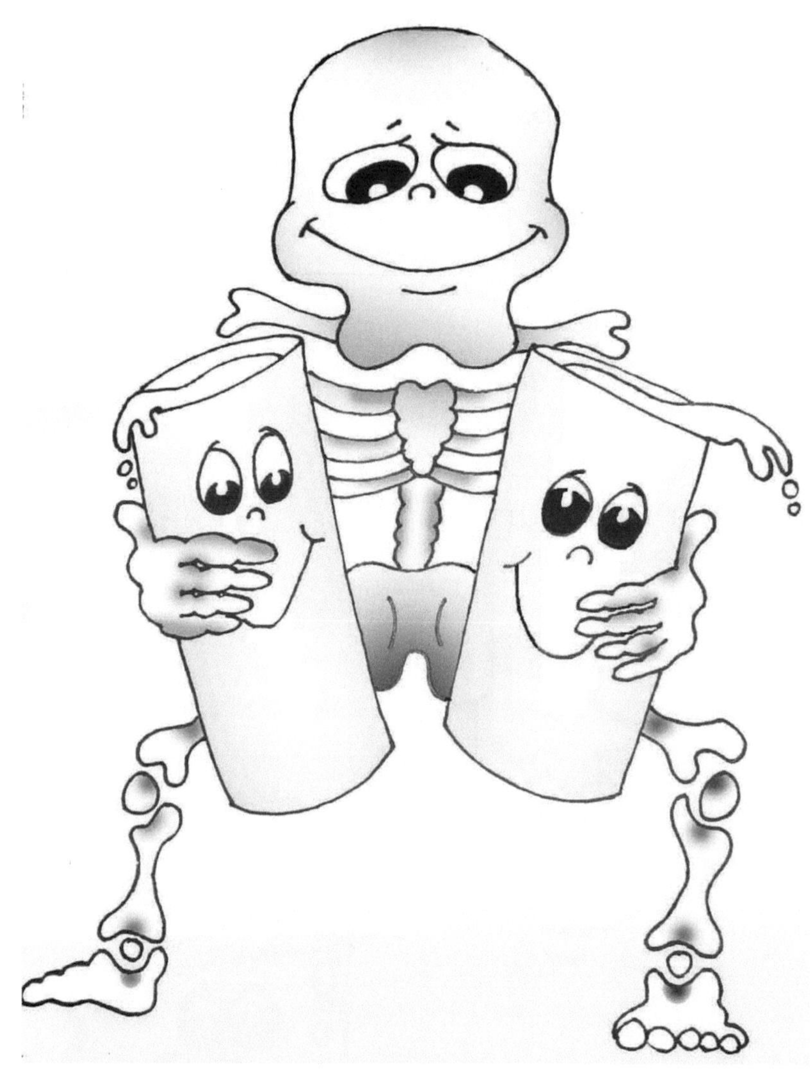

I am a firm food made from milk. I can be white, orange, or yellow. I am eaten with macaroni or crackers. What am I?

(Cheese)

Fun Snack Recipe:

5-Minute Frozen Peach Yogurt

- One 20-oz bag frozen, unsweetened peach slices
- One 8-oz container plain low-fat yogurt
- 2 tablespoons of honey (optional)
- 1 tablespoon of fresh lemon juice
- 1/8 teaspoon almond abstract
- ½ cup of granola

Add peaches to processor. With processor running, add yogurt, honey, lemon juice, almond extract, and granola.

Chapter 5: Meats and Beans Group

All foods made from meats, poultry, fish, dry beans or peas, eggs, nuts, and seeds are considered to be part of this group.

I am white or brown and oval in shape. I come from chickens and you eat me for breakfast. What am I?

(An egg)

How much of this group is needed?

The amount needed depends on your age, gender, and physical activity. The portions below are recommended with thirty minutes or more each day of physical activity beyond your normal daily activities.

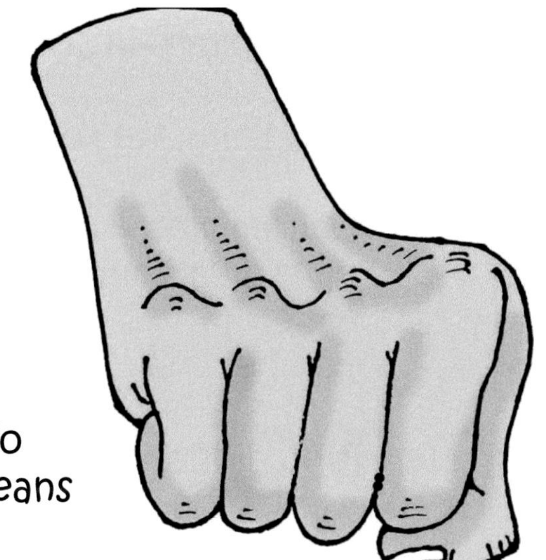

Children 4–8 years old = 3–4 ounces

Girls 9–13 years old = 5 ounces

Boys 9–13 years old = 5 ounces

Eating 5 oz a day of this group with thirty minutes or more of physical activity is good. So what makes up 5 ounces from the meat and beans group?

- 1 oz cooked chicken or fish (e.g., 1 oz canned tuna)
- 1 oz of meat, poultry, or fish (e.g., a slice of turkey)
- ¼ cup of beans
- 1 egg
- 1 tablespoon of peanut butter

For measurement, use your fist as a good 1 oz portion size to measure servings from the meats and beans group. Each item listed can be considered equivalent to one ounce of meats and beans. Combined, these items are considered to be 5 oz of this food group.

I am a very big animal. I fit into a can and make good cracker sandwiches. Some people don't like my smell. I have a very strong smell. What am I?

(Tuna)

Why do I need meats and beans?

Meat, poultry, fish, dry beans and peas, eggs, nuts, and seeds supply nutrients, such as protein, B vitamins, vitamin E, iron, zinc, and magnesium.

- Protein aids in strong bones, muscles, and skin

- B vitamins are for energy release

- E vitamins are antioxidants that help protect your cells against free radicals and or unwanted pollutants

- Iron helps with providing oxygen to the blood

- Zinc aids and supports your immune system (keeps you from getting sick)

- Magnesium helps maintain normal muscle and nerve function, keeps heart rhythm steady, and keeps bones strong.

Fun Snack Recipe:

<u>Turkey Cranberry Roll-Up</u>

- 1 lettuce leaf
- 1 slice of turkey
- 1 low-fat slice of swiss cheese
- Several cranberries

Roll this up together, and there you have it—a turkey cranberry roll-up.

Chapter 6: Oils Group

Oils are fats that are liquid at room temperature, like olive and canola oil, which are used in cooking. Oils come from many different plants, nuts, and fish. Oils contain essential fatty acids that are necessary for good health.

Foods that are mostly oil include mayonnaise, certain salad dressings, and soft margarine with no trans fats.

Chapter 7: Physical Activity

Physical activity simply means movement of the body that releases energy. Jogging, playing soccer, playing basketball, swimming, and dancing are all good examples of being active. Some physical activities are not intense enough to meet recommendations. A good measurement is your heart rate and breathing pattern. If you can say the alphabet without stopping to take a breath directly after your workout, chances are you haven't increased your heart rate.

Why is physical activity important?

Being physically active is a key element to living a longer, healthier, and happier life. Being active helps you manage weight and build and maintain bones, muscles, and joints.

How much activity is needed?

The recommended amount of activity is sixty minutes a day beyond your normal daily activities. Find an activity or sport that moves you. Everyone is different and may like different activities over others. Try new things; don't be afraid. Dive right in; you may love it.
Below is a list of activities that are fun. Choose one, a few, or alternate between all of them.

- Competitive Basketball
- Jump Rope Contest
- Kickball
- Red Light, Green Light
- Rock Wall Climbing
- Relay Race
- Competitive Soccer
- Competitive Football
- Swimming
- Gymnastics
- Karate
- Tennis
- Baseball
- Dancing
- Running

And if those aren't enough fun:

- Be silly; run like a gorilla
- Walk like a spider
- Hop like a bunny
- Stretch like a cat

1. Always eat a variety of foods from the different food groups in the pyramid.

2. Always eat a good breakfast daily.

3. Always eat your fruits and vegetables daily; have at least 5 servings a day.

Life Tips

Food should always be eaten in moderation. Eat your food slowly and in small portions. Wait ten minutes before placing more food on your plate.

Drink more water, drink more water, and drink more water! Up to 80 percent of your body is made of water and we need to drink several glasses a day for proper hydration. A good measurement of water is this: after you go number 1, if the water in the toilet is yellow, you need more water. If you can see through it, your water balance is good. The clearer the water, the better.

Get some sun! We are animals, just like dogs, cats, lions, and tigers. We all need sun and fresh air to grow. Shut off the TV and video games, go outside to play, and socialize with friends. Don't forget to wear your sunscreen.

Always Remember:

Smile and Laugh
Play Hard
Read Books
Do Your Homework
Eat Your Vegetables
Try New Foods
Obey Your Elders
Make Good Grades
Find What Moves You . . . .
Make Friends with Everyone—Girls and Boys
Throw Away Your Trash
Always Say Thank You

Printed in the United States
by Baker & Taylor Publisher Services